HUMAN RIGHTS
AND
FOREIGN POLICY

D1807670

Other Titles of Interest from Pergamon Press

BARNABY, F.
Prospects for Peace

COREA, G.
Need for Change: Towards the New International Economic Order

DAMMANN, E.
The Future in Our Hands

JOLLY, R.
Disarmament and World Development

TAYLOR, R. & PRITCHARD, C.
The Protest Makers: The British Nuclear Disarmament Movement of 1958-1965,
   Twenty Years On

Titles by Evan Luard

The United Nations (1979)

International Agencies (1977)

Conflict and Peace in the Modern International System (1968)

The International Protection of Human Rights (*ed.*) (1968)

Titles Published by the United Nations Association

The United Nations and Human Rights (The UN Department of Public Information;
166 pp., $5)

United States Foreign Policy and Human Rights (1979 Report of the National Policy Panel
of the UNA of the U.S.A.: 86 pp., $3)

Issues before the United Nations (Published each Autumn by the UNA of the U.S.A.;
150 pp., $5)

Protecting Human Rights — Keith D. Suter (1978, UNA of Australia; 44 pp., A$2)

Why the United Nations Association is Important — David J. Harding (U.K. UNA; 34 pp.,
50p)

New World (Periodical of the U.K. United Nations Association, 20p)

The United Nations Association brings together thousands of individuals and hundreds of
organizations, from all sectors of society, to develop the comprehensive world wide co-
operation that is necessary to secure peace and justice. The support we give to the United
Nations is therefore critical and creative. Please join us. Further information about UNA
and the "Human Rights Network" of U.K. organizations is available from any Member or
the Director, UNA, 3 Whitehall Court, London SW1A 2EL (Telephone: 01-930 2931).

HUMAN RIGHTS
AND
FOREIGN POLICY

by

Evan Luard

*(Formerly M.P. for Oxford and Junior
Minister with responsibility for Human
Rights Questions, 1976-1979)*

Published on behalf of the United
Nations Association of Great Britain
and Northern Ireland

by

PERGAMON PRESS

OXFORD · NEW YORK · TORONTO · SYDNEY · PARIS · FRANKFURT

U.K.	Pergamon Press Ltd., Headington Hill Hall, Oxford OX3 0BW, England
U.S.A.	Pergamon Press Inc., Maxwell House, Fairview Park, Elmsford, New York 10523, U.S.A.
CANADA	Pergamon of Canada, Suite 104, 150 Consumers Road, Willowdale, Ontario M2J 1P9, Canada
AUSTRALIA	Pergamon Press (Aust.) Pty. Ltd., P.O. Box 544, Potts Point, N.S.W. 2011, Australia
FRANCE	Pergamon Press SARL, 24 rue des Ecoles, 75240 Paris, Cedex 05, France
FEDERAL REPUBLIC OF GERMANY	Pergamon Press GmbH, 6242 Kronberg-Taunus, Hammerweg 6, Federal Republic of Germany

First edition 1981

British Library Cataloguing in Publication Data

Luard, Evan
Human rights and foreign policy.
1. Civil rights
2. International relations
I. Title II. United Nations Association
323.4   JC571   80-41774

ISBN 0-08-027405-6

*Printed and bound in Great Britain by
William Clowes (Beccles) Limited, Beccles and London*

Foreword

"The Council of the U.K. United Nations Association requests the Executive Committee as a matter of urgency to prepare a UNA policy statement on the role of human rights considerations in determining relations with other states."

Thus read part of a resolution proposed by Martin Ennals at UNA's 1977 General Council in Birmingham. The resolution was passed unanimously . . . obviously. The Executive passed it on to an *ad hoc* committee . . . obviously!

There it stuck. How best can one state help secure human rights in another? We agreed with Dr. David Owen that "the abuse of human rights is the legitimate subject of international concern, and the enforcement of human rights can no longer be left to national governments alone"; but how?

Every argument put forward was matched by another. Sometimes the demands of principle seemed to be winning; sometimes the expediencies of practice. All agreed that every case had to be treated according to its merits . . . but how should those merits be assessed? How could they be assessed by hard-pressed governments?

Who better to help than someone with recent experience in government. So we commissioned the distinguished scholar Evan Luard to examine the papers we had discussed and prepare a reasoned statement.

We are deeply grateful to Mr. Luard for this practical study and to the Joseph Rowntree Charitable Trust, Mr. Robert Maxwell, the Pergamon Press and an anonymous donor for making it possible. Some of it has already "seen the light of day" in the periodical *International Affairs*. Now it is published for government and all those who want to influence foreign policy.

Because this survey concerns "civil and political rights" rather than "economic, social and cultural rights" it is only half the story. No . . . it is a third of the story because eventually the two strands of Human Rights thinking must be interwoven, just as various aspects of Human Rights are interwoven in practice.

Undoubtedly the most extensive suffering in the world is caused by lack of economic rights . . . the death, hunger, disease and illiteracy caused by poverty. Many would say that much of the poverty in the world is caused by the Rich West. Few would deny that the Rich West has so far failed to provide much of a cure for it. So if Western governments want to take Human Rights seriously they must look to better aid, better trade and a better International Economic Order. This is the subject of UNA study, the results of which will be published in another pamphlet to complement this one.

If the publication of this study helps safeguard the human rights of one person it will be worth while. With your help it should be a means of "humanising the system" to the benefit of all humanity.

REVD. DAVID J. HARDING
Director, U.K. United Nations Association

Contents

1 Introduction

There has probably never been a time when there was so much concern about human-rights questions as there is today. Because the world is so much smaller, we are all today more conscious of the human-rights violations that occur in other parts of the world and more determined to do something about them. There is a widespread sentiment that this concern should not simply be voiced by ordinary citizens, or by non-governmental organisations such as UNA and Amnesty, but should be expressed in the foreign policy of governments. Foreign policies, in other words, should not just be concerned with the promotion of narrow, national self-interest but with remedying the injustices suffered by many in other countries living under tyrannical and inhumane governments. If government policies reflect the deep concern of their citizens on this issue, the means available to governments, and to governments alone, can be brought into play and help to influence the policies being pursued by other governments towards their own populations, and to end, or at least reduce, the grievous violations of rights which many continue to suffer.

During the last two or three years there have been more active efforts by governments in a number of Western countries to implement such policies. The Carter administration in the United States and the former Labour government in this country each sought to pursue active policies in this field. Some smaller countries, such as Sweden and the Netherlands, have made similar attempts. The policies of these governments were designed not only to make general statements about the importance of respect for human rights, but to take actions related to individual countries to induce them to change their policies. Where these have failed, there have been adjustments of policy—withdrawal of ambassadors, or the cutting off of aid—as an indication of the importance attached to these matters.

1

Both the Carter administration in the United States and the former Labour government here have been criticised for their efforts in this field. These criticisms have been made mainly on two diametrically opposed grounds. They were attacked by some for failing to pursue the policies with sufficient vigour and outspokenness, especially where to do so would threaten other foreign-policy aims (for example, so it was said, in the cases of Iran and Saudi Arabia or even in those of South Africa and the Soviet Union). By others they were criticised for injecting into inter-state relations highly controversial issues relating to the internal affairs of other states, which therefore aroused the maximum resentment and hostility among such states, without even succeeding in influencing the situations in those countries significantly: this, it was said, prejudiced the attainment of other objectives in the foreign-policy field which might have been otherwise achieved and which were more vital to the interests of the Western countries concerned.

This is thus a good moment to look again at these difficult questions and to consider how much weight should be attached to these criticisms and what lessons, if any, may be learnt about what governments can achieve by their efforts in this area.

There is nothing new in concern among governments about human-rights matters. Questions concerning freedom, the right to a fair trial, the rule of law, freedom from torture or arbitrary imprisonment, the right of assembly, freedom of speech and so on, all these have been the stuff of politics within states almost since states began. Even concern about the enjoyment of such rights in *other* states goes back two centuries at least, to the beginning of the agitation over slavery and the slave trade in the late eighteenth century. The question of the role of human-rights issues in foreign policy has been discussed for well over a century (for example, in the controversy over Gladstone's famous Midlothian campaign, when he challenged the response of the Disraeli government to Turkish atrocities in Bosnia and Bulgaria).

Yet it is undoubtedly the case that over recent years the enjoyment of human rights elsewhere has been a more significant preoccupation of governments, or at least of some governments, in the prosecution of their foreign policy than in any earlier times. The main reason for this is undoubtedly that we know more about what happens in neighbouring countries and we care more in consequence. Populations are more concerned on such questions and influence governments to be so too. At the same time there exist now for the first time institutions—such as the UN Commission on Human Rights and the European Commission and Court of European Rights—that are directly concerned with those problems; these provide the opportunity to discuss such questions at least, so that governments must formulate their policies to take part in discussions. For these reasons human rights policy has become a more central feature of foreign policy than at any earlier time. Governments need to establish the principles that should guide their conduct.

The desire of a government to play an active role in this field, however, encounters immediate difficulties. Its concern to make an issue of human-rights violations in some other country may conflict with other important foreign policy aims. Thus President Carter, for example, has been rightly concerned with the pursuit of détente with the Soviet Union; and he has found that the attainment of that objective has sometimes compelled him to be more restrained about the treatment of dissidents in the Soviet Union than he showed himself in his first years of office. The Labour government found that Britain's close economic involvement with South Africa sometimes constrained it to be cautious towards proposals for international action against that country which might involve economic sanctions. Both the United States and Britain, for all their genuine concern about the human-rights policies of the Shah of Iran, felt compelled by economic and strategic interests to speak out on his behalf even in his dying days of power. While he was still Foreign Secretary David Owen accepted that, because of foreign-policy considerations of this kind, there could not be complete consistency in the policies adopted: political factors also sometimes play a part. On these grounds both governments were, partly for political reasons, considerably more severe with Chile than with Argentina, even though the situation in the latter country has in the last two or three years certainly been far worse.

These are typical of the conflicts of interest that are always likely to be encountered (and to be seized on by critics) when such policies are pursued, even when governments are genuinely and sincerely committed to seeking improvements in the human-rights situation all over the world (and few serious observers would doubt that President Carter and the last Labour administration were serious in their attempts in that direction). Any government that seeks to commit itself to such a policy is bound to find itself faced by difficult choices and to encounter serious constraints which appear to limit its freedom of action. It must be one of our purposes in this paper to examine how serious these constraints really are.

2 Foreign Policy Constraints on Human-Rights Policy

What then is the nature of the constraints?

First, all governments need to have dealings with almost every other government of the world, whether it approves of them or not, on many diverse questions. It must deal with them over the welfare of its own nationals resident in that country, or trading there; over commercial and other matters between the two states; over many practical problems affecting both states; over any aid programme it may be implementing; and over many wider issues affecting the international community as a whole. It will deal with them both bilaterally and in the UN and other international organisations. Such dealings are designed (as Winston Churchill said about the act of recognition) "not to confer a compliment but to secure a convenience". An active campaign designed to denounce the domestic policies of such a government will inevitably arouse deep resentment and will complicate dealings on any practical matter between the two states. It may endanger commercial or other prospects and the securing of government contracts. It will certainly damage political goodwill (about which our embassies abroad are often mainly concerned). And since it will not necessarily bring any improvement in the human-rights situation in the country concerned in any case, it is understandable that many governments are reluctant to stick their necks out on such issues (and are nearly always advised by their representatives on the spot not to do so).

In some cases there may be more special reasons why it is believed inadvisable to antagonise the other government concerned. That state may be considered important for strategic reasons; may even be an ally, so that to engage in criticisms which might endanger the government's position may be held to be highly undesirable on defence grounds: it was these considerations which are believed by many to have muted criticisms among other NATO governments of the Salazar regime in Portugal and that of the colonels in Greece in former days, as well as some other governments in other parts of the world. Or the state concerned may be an important commercial partner: the consideration which is sometimes said to have damped down British criticisms of Iran, Argentina and other states in recent years. It may be an important supplier of raw materials: as South Africa is to all Western countries. It may be a financially powerful state which could make its displeasure felt in the foreign exchange markets; a consideration which some believe to have virtually silenced criticism of Saudi Arabia and other oil-producing states in recent years. Finally, it may be a great power with which negotiations on many delicate subjects, including vital strategic issues, are being undertaken: thus, for example, the conclusion of a Salt agreement with the Soviet Union was regarded by some as so important as to deter too outspoken criticisms of her human rights policies by the United States.

A third kind of argument that can be used against attempts to undertake an active human-rights policy is that it is contrary to the rules of diplomatic intercourse. The tradition that each state exercises full sovereignty within its own territory and that other states therefore should not interfere in such matters is firmly established and is said to reduce the danger of conflict among states through mutual interference. This rule, it is sometimes held, precludes any criticism of the actions of other governments within their own countries. International bodies, such critics claim, are equally debarred from interfering in such matters: Article 2(7) of the U.N. Charter states that nothing in the Charter "shall authorise the United Nations to intervene in matters which are essentially within the domestic jurisdiction of any state". These rules, even if they are not always accepted by those nations which wish to make the criticisms, will certainly be insisted on by those that are under criticism (as, for example, British governments of all political persuasions have consistently rejected the right of foreign governments or organisations, and even of foreign commentators, to make judgements on British policy in Northern Ireland). How much more, it is argued, will authoritarian governments, often guilty of gross brutality towards their own subjects, reject any attempt by outsiders to influence their conduct? If every government began criticising and commenting on all action of every other government in every part of the world, even undertaken within their own territories, offering perhaps conflicting advice, the conduct of international affairs would, under this view, become impossible. Is it not far wiser, it is asked, to maintain the traditional rules on this question and so reduce the possible areas of conflict?

Finally, the fourth type of argument often used against governments taking too active a role on these matters is that such efforts are in any case ineffectual: they will have no influence. They are thus a waste of energy, resources, and political capital. The type of government that engages in this oppression of basic human freedoms, it is said, is often already intensely insecure in its internal position and is unlikely to be deterred from its policies by outside criticism. Indeed for such a government it may be a point of honour to ignore all criticisms to demonstrate its own dependence and its unwillingness to be deterred: so, some hold, the Western campaigns on behalf of dissidents in the Soviet Union do not in fact alter Soviet policy on that question and only make it more difficult for the Soviet Government to make the concessions which it might otherwise be willing to grant and so intensify the possibility that harsh penalties may be imposed as a demonstration that that government cannot be deflected from its chosen course by outside criticism. Outside condemnation might, by attracting publicity to the affair, even cause a government to behave more toughly than would otherwise be the case, to show that it cannot be intimidated. Finally, it is argued that overt criticisms on such questions, by alienating the government concerned, may in fact serve to *reduce* the influence of outside governments which make them, and make it less likely that they can have any useful impact in similar situations in the future.

The force and influence of all these different arguments should not be underestimated by those who are concerned about human-rights questions. All of them may be challenged: and we will in the next section look at the weaknesses of some of them. But they are none of them altogether irrational. And the important point is that, whether or not they are true, they are *believed* by many governments and so deter attempts at least by governments to pursue an active policy in this field (none of the arguments of course apply to activity by unofficial organisations). The objections are ones that therefore have to be considered carefully.

Let us, before going on to consider what governments can and should do, look at each of them in a little more detail and consider the amount of weight that needs to be attached to them.

3 How Important are these Constraints?

The first argument we described suggested that, because governments have to deal with each other all the time on a wide variety of issues, they cannot risk exacerbating their relations by injecting controversial issues of human-rights policy which will inevitably cause grave offence and may even fatally damage relations in every field, so endangering other important ends or policy.

It is of course the case that governments are at all times obliged to deal on a day-to-day basis with many governments whether or not it approves of them, on a large number of different and mainly uncontroversial issues. Most of these relations will continue whatever posture one government may adopt on human-rights issues. The argument we described has force only if it is assumed that expressions of concern by one government on human-rights questions will totally prejudice the conduct of normal business with the government that is criticised. But there is little evidence for this assumption. It is unreasonable to expect that relations will be totally unaffected. But the *degree* to which relations are damaged will depend partly on other factors governing the relationship between the two states, and it will depend even more on the manner in which the issue is raised. If the complaints made are aired in a polemical and highly political style, or are pursued obsessively and to the exclusion of all other questions, the relationship may indeed be seriously damaged. If, on the other hand, the complaint made is raised in the proper forum, in reasonable terms, and is consistent with the policy pursued on similar matters towards other states, this need not be the case. If the issue has been raised first on a confidential basis, and without publicity, the government concerned will be given notice in advance that the matter is one which genuinely arouses strong feelings and will be less surprised if it is subsequently raised in a public forum. Similarly if the charges made are specific, factual and backed by firm evidence, rather than vague and generalised, it will have less justification for any belief or accusation that they are inspired by malice or political prejudice. Perhaps the most important condition is that of consistency. If Western governments (as in the early cold war years) denounced only human-rights violations in Eastern Europe, but ignore those of their allies in the West; if communist states denounced the situation in Chile or Northern Ireland, but say nothing of that in Cuba or Ethiopia, they cannot expect to be treated as unbiased in such campaigns.

The fact that human-rights issues have already in the last few years become so much the normal stuff of international politics has reduced the danger that any expression of concern on such matters can be used by other governments as a justification of breaking off or damaging relations. Not only Western countries but many developing states as well have become increasingly active over such issues and play a growing role in the international bodies responsible. The development of new institutions with responsibility in this area, both at the world level (the UN Commission on Human Rights, and its sub-Commissions) and at the regional level (the European and Inter-American Commissions) and the increasingly active role these bodies play, has accentuated this trend. No individual government can any longer insulate itself altogether from this change in the international climate. Even the Soviet Union today submits to questioning on its domestic policies in the Human Rights Committee (which supervises the implementation of the Covenant on Civil and Political rights). She and nearly all other states gladly participate elsewhere in the discussion of the human-rights policies of South African, Chilean and Israeli governments, and rightly reject any attempt by the governments of those countries to claim immunity on the grounds of domestic sovereignty. It is thus almost universally recognised that serious violations of human rights are a matter of concern to the international community as a whole and, while the states accused will doubtless continue to protest when other governments criticise their record, it is less and less likely that inter-state relations will be fatally damaged because one state dares to criticise the performance of another in this field, so long as it does so in the appropriate matter.

All the evidence of recent years confirms this fact. Even the governments that are most fiercely criticised do not in practice fatally disrupt relationships in retaliation. Even at the time when U.S. criticisms of Soviet human rights policies were at their height, the Soviet Union continued to discuss Salt and many other matters as before. Similarly, criticisms of South Africa's policies of apartheid or Israel's policies in occupied territories have not prevented the governments which have made them from maintaining relatively normal relations with those governments on other questions. There is, in other words, a considerable willingness to divorce disagreements on such matters from the conduct of affairs in other areas. It cannot, of course, be said that no price will be paid for being outspoken: this is the cost of having a human-rights policy. But it is not usually an unduly heavy one. And in general, therefore, the first of the four objections which we listed against an active human-rights policy is not one that can be considered to have overwhelming weight.

The second objection to an active policy on human rights which we described concerned the special difficulty which arises when human-rights violations occur in states which have a particular importance, whether diplomatic, strategic or commercial. Thus it is argued that, even if Western governments can afford to be outspoken in condemning a remote and insignificant state in Africa or Asia whose goodwill is unimportant, they should be less uninhibited in their public criticism of states which are their close allies, or which have the power of life or death for their economies, or even those on which they are negotiating over important strategic questions.

The first thing to be said about this is that if this is the objection to an active human-rights policy, such a policy can still be pursued towards the great majority of states, which do not fall into any of these categories. But even in the other cases, the argument is open to challenge. It is, for example, often the case that where there is a special relationship with a particular country of this kind, it is a reciprocal one: the government being criticised may attach quite as much importance to that relationship as the one that is doing the criticising. In these circumstances even though the former may be resentful of criticism, it will have in practice no alternative but to accept it and will be most unlikely to take actions that are seriously damaging to its partners. This is why the suggestions made at the time that Western states could not afford to be too rude to the former regimes of Salazar in Portugal or the colonels in Greece or the Shah of Iran, were so specious and short-sighted. For those governments were in fact far more dependent on the good-will of the West than the West was on them. Thus the blood-curdling stories sometimes peddled in such situations—that if we antagonise such governments they may suddenly abandon us and go over to the "enemy"—lack all credibility. The fact is that such regimes usually (as in all these cases) have nowhere else to go. They are tied firmly into their existing alliances, both by strong ideological conviction and by prudent self-interest (it is more a matter for question how far the West can really gain, even in purely strategic terms, from allies whose policies are so questionable and who are therefore so vulnerable to political overthrow). It might rather be argued that the fact that such countries are allies gives Western states both a greater right and a greater incentive in seeking to bring about the changes in such regimes which alone can make them acceptable and durable partners.

Still less is it true that Western governments cannot afford to offend powerful adversaries such as the Soviet Union. Salt negotiations may not have been helped by President Carter's public comments on the Soviet Government's treatment of dissidents, but they were certainly not stopped. It was always unlikely that they would have been since détente and Salt ratification is at least as much in the interests of the Soviet Union as of the West. Nor are important oil producers, such as Saudi Arabia, likely suddenly to halt their oil supplies, or double the price, because they are angered by criticisms of their domestic policies. For their policies too are determined ultimately by their own conception of their economic self-interest, and it is improbable that their calculations in this respect would be significantly altered by comments from Western states concerning their domestic policies.

It is thus far less the case than is often suggested that governments must constantly maintain a prudent silence about the policies of other states which are important to them. Provided, once more, criticisms are raised in a reasonable and unpolemical manner, reactions are unlikely to be so drastic as is occasionally suggested. Again the evidence of the past supports this. Although the Shah of Iran was frequently strongly criticised in Western countries, and occasionally even by Western governments, he was not in any way deterred from his pro-Western allegiance, nor at any time considered cutting off oil or raising its price on such grounds. While the Arab oil-producing countries cut off oil to two states for a time in 1973, this was because of those states' alleged sympathy with Israel, not because of offence at Western comments on their own affairs. Nigeria nationalised British oil in that country in 1979; but this was said to be a reaction to Britain's policies concerning Rhodesia, not to comments on the human-rights situation in Nigeria. The fact is that governments today have come to expect comment on human-rights affairs by other states; and there is no evidence that they will wantonly sacrifice the relations that are most important to them by overreacting to expressions of concern which, however unwelcome to them, can never be a fatal threat to their vital interests.

The reason that governments generally refrain from speaking out on such questions is because it is inconvenient to do so, not because it is fatally damaging. It is not believed to be worthwhile to create difficulties in relations with important states for ends that are regarded, by most officials and by many ministers, as only marginal in importance. How far a government will in practice go in criticising a friendly or politically important state about its human-rights policies depends usually on the degree to which public opinion at home demands it, rather than on the absolute scale of its atrocities. British governments have not hesitated to express their condemnation of policies of, for example, the Soviet Union, Uganda, Chile and South Africa, because public opinion at home demanded it. They spoke out less strongly about the policies of Equatorial Guinea, the Central African Republic, Argentina, Cuba and China, because British public opinion and even British human-rights organisations have not expressed themselves as strongly in those cases, not because it was thought important not to prejudice relations with those states.

The third difficulty we noted against making human-rights considerations a prominent element in foreign policy was that the pursuit of human-rights aims by governments (as against unofficial organisations) is contrary to the traditional rules of diplomatic intercourse forbidding interference in internal affairs. Here the simple answer is that the rules of diplomatic intercourse change all the time, and have changed quite dramatically in the last thirty or forty years. Such a change was already manifested in the United Nations Charter, in which provision was explicitly made for the discussion of human-rights matters in the organisation, and in its Commission on Human Rights in particular. This has been reinforced by the subsequent establishment of regional organisations devoted to the same subject, such as the European Commission and Court of Human Rights and the Inter-American Commission on Human Rights, and subsequently in such documents as the Helsinki Final Act, which has clear references to human-rights issues. And it is shown above all in the current practice of states many of which (not all developed countries) continually make clear the importance they attach to the conduct of other governments in this respect.

Nor are these arguments overcome by referring to traditional conceptions of "sovereignty" or to Article 2(7) of the UN Charter already quoted. For definitions of the sovereign rights of states, or of what is "essentially within the domestic jurisdiction" of a state, as the Charter puts it, are continually evolving. So is the definition of "intervene" in that context. Today there are few states that consider it inadmissible for another government to express concern about human-rights issues in *general*; while many accept that this carries with it the implication that governments must sometimes express concern about the human-rights situation in particular states. International law has never been a static and inflexible body of rules. And it is perhaps in this particular area that it has evolved most rapidly in recent years.

The final argument we noted against a government playing too active a role in this field was that such policies are anyway ineffective. Few governments are influenced by public expressions of concern on such matters, it is said, and may only be incited to worse excesses. But this argument is contrary to the facts. There are a considerable number of cases where international pressures, including public expressions of concern by other governments, have led to significant improvements in the human-rights policies of particular states. In recent years this has occurred, for example, in Chile, Indonesia, Iran, Brazil, and probably in Argentina. Even in the Soviet Union there is evidence that on some matters—for example the emigration of Jewish people—policy has been significantly altered because of hostile comment from elsewhere.

But this criticism anyway misconceives the effect that is ultimately to be expected from the actions of government in this field. For few realistic observers expect that, because one or two governments begin to state their concern about the human-rights situation in a particular state (say Uganda or Equatorial Guinea), the government of that country is suddenly going to reverse all its policies and become all at once a model of virtue. In the short term, little may happen. But there may be a number of indirect effects. First the government under attack, whether or not it undergoes a change of heart, may be gradually brought to realise that there are significant external costs to the type of policy it is pursuing. At least its foreign office, which is usually most aware of foreign criticisms, may become an influence within the government machine for a reform of policy. Secondly, human-rights campaigners within the country concerned may be given new hope and encouragement, and redouble their own efforts to secure reforms. Changes may be induced within the government itself, with those favouring a more liberal policy (partly because of its foreign-policy effects) prevailing over those furthering repressive policies (as occurred for a time in South Korea). But above all, it is the international climate as a whole which will be altered by expressions of concern on such matters. The expectations that are placed on all members of the international community are slowly changed. New norms of the behaviour to be expected from civilised governments are established. Regional organisations, that may have previously been ineffective in this field, may become more active. It is this wider effect, the slowest and most indirect of all, which may none the less ultimately be the most important in reducing the scale of human-rights violations. For ultimately it will affect the expectations and attitudes of all: even those of future governments which might otherwise be tempted towards tyrannical policies.

Thus none of the arguments that have been put forward against an active human-rights policy are convincing. This does not mean that the arguments should be discounted altogether. It must be accepted that there are real difficulties for any government in carrying out a firm and consistent human-rights policy. It will on occasion appear to conflict with other foreign-policy aims, whether it is accommodation with a super-power, the cultivation of relations with an influential third world country, or even the maximising of exports. What is suggested here is not that such choices never have to be made. It is that the conflict is not as acute as is often made out. Relative frankness on human-rights issues is normally compatible with the achievement of other foreign-policy goals. Equally important, even where a direct choice has to be made, the human-rights objective, in a world where very serious human-rights violations still occur, ought in many cases to prevail (put differently there are costs in not responding to human-rights violations). But this requires courage among governments. If, where such a choice is necessary, governments continually take the easy way out, convince themselves that here is a special case, that relations with such and such an important country cannot be put at risk, the entire policy begins to be valueless. It ceases to be an attempt to act in accordance with certain moral principles and becomes a policy of expediency, to be applied only where it conforms with other foreign-policy objectives.

To make such a policy successful, therefore, requires consistency and toughness. No foreign-policy objective can be achieved without a price. The saving of lives elsewhere, the prevention of torture and other violations of essential liberties, may be a goal for which it is sometimes worth paying such a price.

4 The Ends of Human-Rights Policy

If it is accepted that the concern that is now widely felt over human rights should be reflected in foreign policy, what are the precise objectives such a policy should try to achieve, and how should it set about achieving them?

The first distinction to be made is between the general and the particular. Policy will be concerned in part to secure *general* recognition of the importance of human rights all over the world and to define precisely what are the rights that all governments should protect. And in part policy will be concerned with preventing or deterring *particular* violations of rights in individual countries in all parts of the world. Both of these have their part to play and neither can be ignored. Unless general principles are clearly laid down and widely publicised, governments cannot even know what is expected of them, nor is there a standard by which to judge their policies. Conversely, there is no value in establishing general principles in abstract form, unless a real attempt is also made to ensure that they are observed in practice. Until recently most of the energies of the international community were devoted to the former task. And it could be said that there now exists a fairly broad set of general statements of principle, setting out the main rights which the international community demands should be protected. The latter task—ensuring that these principles are observed—is by far the more difficult, partly for the reasons we have considered in the previous section. But it is to this that the world community needs to devote the greatest attention today.

Let us first seek to suggest briefly the main objectives to be pursued by governments in this field, before going on to look at the way they can best be attained. The first aim of any government that is deeply concerned in these issues, I would suggest, is to ensure that human-rights concerns remain constantly at the top, or near the top, of the international agenda. The easiest policy to pursue in this field is to remain silent. Because human rights are a controversial question, and because discussion of them must cause the sparks to fly, governments are inevitably tempted to conclude that discretion is the better part of

15

valour and simply keep quiet on the subject. Because governments deal with other governments, the temptation is not to offend them too much, whatever the shortcomings in their conduct. But if the question is as important as many people believe, and if governments can have an influence that other groups cannot, then it is essential that governments, as well as unofficial organisations, continue to make human rights an important international issue and ensure that they are publicly discussed. And if, as I have suggested, it is the entire climate of international opinion which has most influence in determining the policies pursued by governments, it is essential that those governments which are concerned on such questions continually raise it to the forefront of attention in order to influence the attitudes and expectations of others.

A second important aim of human-rights policy must be to ensure that the minimum standards of human rights which civilised states expect to see observed are satisfactorily defined. Here a considerable amount of progress has already been made by the international bodies responsible over the last thirty or forty years. The essential standards governments should observe were first laid down, in somewhat general terms, in the Universal Declaration of Human Rights, formulated more than thirty years ago and endorsed by almost the entire international community. Since then these have been amplified in more detailed and specific instruments, mainly formulated in the UN Commission on Human Rights. The most important of these are perhaps the two Covenants on civil and political rights and on economic, social and cultural rights respectively, the former of which has now come into effect. There are also more specialised instruments covering particular fields, such as the Convention on All Forms of Racial Discrimination, and that still being discussed on religious tolerance. There are also special regional codes such as those established in the European Convention and applied by the European Commission and Court of Human Rights, and that operated by the Inter-American Commission on Human Rights. One of the continuing aims of governments working in this field is to clarify and amplify this code, particularly by extending it in certain specialised areas.

A third aim of policy must be to ensure that better machinery exists to try to see that the new codes are complied with. It is of no value laying down general principles if these principles continue to be flouted by large numbers of governments, including many that have in theory subscribed to these documents. It is generally accepted that the UN bodies responsible should now move on from legislation to the process often described as "implementation": ensuring that governments adequately conform with the good intentions which they have professed. Improvement of the machinery to achieve this is by no means easy, because of the resistances that exist among large parts of the membership to granting the UN effective powers in this field. This results partly from a general sensitivity about sovereignty, a reluctance to see any interference by international bodies in domestic matters. And it results partly from the fact that many governments have skeletons in their own cupboards and recognise that if more effective machinery were created it could well be applied against themselves.

The fourth and most important aim of human-rights policy must be to bring direct influence on governments all over the world so that the grave violation of human rights which today are unhappily still only too common are less likely to occur. As we have seen, this is both the most important and the most difficult task. Governments are often as indifferent to the representations of individual governments as to the recommendations of international bodies. Often they may believe that their own survival depends on the continuation of policies of repression, that they face a "security" problem which requires that "subversive" forces should be suppressed. In these circumstances, even if they recognise that serious violations of human rights are occurring, they may feel that these are the inevitable cost of maintaining power, or bringing a disturbed situation under control (this has, for instance, been the main justification used for human-rights violations in Argentina, Uruguay and some other Latin American countries in recent times). Or, even worse, they may, like an Amin or a Pol Pot, care absolutely nothing for the opinions of other countries, any more than they do for that of their own people, and thus appear almost totally impervious to any representations or appeals that other states may make. But whatever the motives or attitudes of such governments, it is an essential aim of human-rights policy to bring effective influence to bear to secure a reversal of policy.

This is not an exclusive list of the human-rights aims which a

Western government concerned with such matters will wish to pursue. But it probably includes the main objectives that governments will have in mind. Let us now go on therefore to consider the more difficult question, what are the *means* by which such objectives can best be achieved?

5 The Means of Human-Rights Policy

The first of the aims I have mentioned—ensuring that human rights remains near the top of the international agenda—is perhaps the easiest to achieve. No government has any reason to feel inhibited from declaring in general terms its concern on this question. The supreme achievement of President Carter in this field has not been the changes he has brought about in individual countries (which must surely be less than he had hoped): it is that he has publicly demonstrated the importance that he and his government attach to the question of human rights, and has made it part of the normal subject-matter of relations between states. It will be a tragedy if any failings in the particular application of this policy—and, as we have noted, there have been successes as well as failures—should cause any move to back-track on that general aim. It is thus essential that the present British and other Western governments should continue to show their support for that general objective and should continue to make clear the importance they too attach to performance in this field. Only if other governments in all parts of the world are clearly aware that they are being judged, by their friends as well as by their opponents, partly on the basis of their performance in this respect, is their behaviour likely to be influenced. Only if the importance which civilised states attach to the preservation of elementary human rights, even in poor states, is continually reaffirmed, will the necessary international climate be established and the attitude of governments and populations alike be gradually transformed.

It is sometimes suggested that Western countries, in the insistent emphasis they place on human-rights matters, are, at least in their dealings with Third World states, seeking to impose on countries of totally different cultures and conditions attitudes and standards developed in the West for Western societies which are in no way appropriate to them. It is held that there are no absolute standards in this field, and that it is only comparatively recently that Western countries themselves have begun to conform with the principles which they now preach so ardently. They thus have no right to seek to apply them to others of widely differing backgrounds. For poor countries, it is said, human rights begin with breakfast. What matters to them is that people should have enough to eat and to house and clothe their families. The civil and political liberties to which Western countries attach such importance, therefore, are a luxury and an irrelevance which have little meaning for such countries.

The argument is a gross and unwarranted insult to the poor countries that it purports to defend. When we speak of human rights we are speaking of the elementary right of people not to be killed, not to be tortured, not to be arbitrarily imprisoned, not to be raped or assaulted. Those rights are not a recent discovery: they have been recognised the world over almost from the beginning of time. The belief in such rights is not the invention of the Western world but is cherished equally in the Third World. There are a considerable number of poor countries (particularly in the Pacific, in the Caribbean and parts of Africa and Asia) which have consistently maintained the very highest standards of human rights despite a very low standard of living (just as there have been some wealthy countries that have none the less extremely poor records in this respect). But if it is an insult to the governments and people of those countries which have good records to suggest that human-rights standards should not be applied to poor countries, it is even more of an insult to the hundreds of thousands, and possibly millions, who have suffered violations of their rights, who have lost their lives in Cambodia and Uganda, or been tortured in Latin America, to imply, however indirectly, that the governments of such countries cannot be expected to refrain from killing or torturing them because of the low standard of living there. Arguments on these lines indeed—apart from being factually false—could be used to provide a heaven-sent justification to tyrants and petty officials or military officers in poor countries who wish to find excuses for their repressive policies. It is not the case—and fortunately is not accepted as the case in most developing countries—that poverty excuses or condones barbarous conduct by governments there.

Nor is there, as such arguments imply, in some way a choice to be made between economic rights and civil rights. Both sets of rights are of the highest importance. But they are in no way in conflict with each other. Development is not impeded in a society which respects human rights. On the contrary, what evidence we have shows that it is assisted. In general some of the developing countries which have shown the highest respect for human rights have the best record of economic growth (Ivory Coast, Venezuela, Malaysia, for example). And conversely it is in states where human rights have been most widely and systematically abused—in such countries as Cambodia, Equatorial Guinea, the Central African Republic, Haiti, Uruguay and Paraguay, for example—that economic growth has been slowest (if it has not indeed been backward).

The two types of rights, therefore, far from being in conflict are complementary. It is the governments that are genuinely concerned about the economic standard of living of their people that usually have most concern about their rights in other fields as well; while conversely it is those that are least concerned about their civil rights that will neglect their economic rights likewise. It is a legitimate argument for Third World countries to use against the West that, if they are concerned about human rights at all, they should be concerned about economic rights as well (and therefore be willing to provide more aid or better access to their markets). It is not a legitimate argument that, because economic rights are important, civil rights can be ignored.

Fortunately this is a truth generally recognized by most Third World countries. And nothing has been more heartening during recent years than to note the importance attached to this subject by many Third World countries and to see the leading role played in the Human Rights Commission (for example) by a number of Third World states (such as Senegal, Nigeria, Sierra Leone, Jordan and India). Indeed there is a case for saying that Western countries should, so far as possible—to avoid the charge of a neo-colonialist paternalism—leave to other Third World countries the task of highlighting the violations that occur in parts of the Third World. The standards they apply, however, will be those that are generally applied to the international community as a whole. It is not by chance that the most important international instrument in this field is entitled the *Universal* Declaration of Human Rights, and was adopted without a single dissentient vote. The assertion was that the standards laid down could and should be attained in any country. It was never accepted that any state is too small, too remote or too poor to be expected to attain them.

The second general aim we mentioned was to carry forward the process of defining and elaborating the responsibilities of states in assuring the protection of human rights. Here the means required to achieve this are well established and no revolutionary changes are needed. Since any convention or other instrument in this field must, if it is to have any influence, reflect the views of the international community generally, it can only emerge from a process of international negotiation as at present. There may be room for improving the procedures used for this purpose. At present the work is done sometimes by working groups of the Commission on Human Rights or (as in the case of the Covenants) by the Commission itself, followed by detailed examination in the Third Committee of the General Assembly. It cannot really be said that such bodies, with fairly low-level representatives often with little or no legal background, are well equipped for this difficult but very important task. It really requires a forum that is legal rather than political in its approach. There is a case for asking the International Law Commission (which is anyway less directly representative of governments) to be more closely involved in the process in the future. The Commission, composed of distinguished international lawyers from a balanced group of countries, though it has undertaken the drafting of a number of extremely important conventions, has not taken any part in drafting conventions in the field of human rights. Since it is balanced by nationality, like all UN bodies, it reflects as well as they do the varying national approaches to such questions. But it will not be so influenced by narrowly political factors as purely intergovernmental bodies sometimes are.

In the immediate future the most important need is the drafting of a satisfactory convention on the subject of torture, on which discussion is now taking place. There are also important debates concerning new rules governing the rights of mental patients (it is well known that it is a common practice in certain countries to incarcerate troublesome dissidents by declaring them mentally disordered); as well as rules governing the treatment of all those under detention. All of these are vitally important questions—central issues for the protection of human rights—and it is vital that satisfactory texts should be achieved which can significantly influence the behaviour of governments in these areas. It is particularly important that there should be a satisfactory international convention covering torture, one of the most hideous yet most widely used violations of human rights in recent years, and that such a convention is widely ratified. But efforts to improve penal practice generally are also required. Although, for example, imprisonment without trial is often regarded as one of the most serious violations of human rights that can occur it is widespread; and there are many countries all over the world, including some with otherwise good human-rights records (such as India and Italy), where people, subsequently found to be perfectly innocent, may languish in jail for many years before being brought to trial at all.

The third objective we named for a constructive human-rights policy was the improvement of the international machinery which at present exists for promoting and protecting such rights. Foreign policy concerning human rights must be partly a policy for improving this machinery. However committed its government and however active in this field, Britain can do little, acting bilaterally, to secure more effective protection of rights elsewhere. One of our aims, if we are concerned to make progress in this field, must, therefore, be to secure better *international* action to bring this about.

At present the main body concerned is the UN Commission on Human Rights. Though it has been criticised with some reason in the past, there has been some significant improvement in the operation of this body in recent years. It has come to recognise that what really counts is deeds and not words, and that therefore what is now required is better machinery to ensure that governments abide by their undertakings. This has been shown in two ways. When new instruments have neen negotiated it has been laid down from the start in one or two cases that there should be some machinery for supervising implementation. This was true of the Convention for the Elimination of Racial Discrimination (1965); and, more importantly, for the

Covenant on Civil and Political Rights which came into effect in 1976. In both cases inter-governmental committees have been set up which cross-examine representatives of each government on their performance in putting the instrument into effect, and subsequently issue a report. The necessity to justify themselves before these committees, and the danger of being exposed when it has been shown they are flagrantly failing to live up to their obligations probably represent some influence on governments (as do the similar procedures employed by the ILO over many years for covenants concerning labour standards). Minorities within the state concerned are also able to quote the terms of the undertaking which their government has made. And the procedures serve to establish more unmistakably than written documents alone the standards of national conduct which are expected by the international community.

The other, and perhaps more important, development is the use of the so-called 1503 procedure (named after the ECOSOC resolution which first established it). This is a procedure under which the human-rights situation in particular countries may be examined by the Commission. The procedure is long and cumbrous, beginning in a Working Group of the Sub-Commission (that meets in August/September); goes from them to the Sub-Commission, which may and often does recommend action by the Commission. It then goes to another Working Group of the Commission itself; which finally makes a further recommendation to the Commission. The number of hurdles to be crossed has meant that very few issues have got all the way through to substantive discussion and decision by the Commission. Moreover, all the discussion is, at least in theory, confidential: though in practice there are often judicious leaks at least about which countries have been discussed (so that the procedure may begin to have an effect even if it never reaches its final conclusion). However, public discussion is also possible by other procedures. The situation in Chile, South Africa and the territories occupied by Israel have all been discussed publicly. The former Labour government in Britain raised the situations in Uganda and Cambodia in public debate in the Commission; and in both cases eventually some form of international action ensued, though it is symptomatic of the very slow-moving machinery that in each case the offending government was overthrown before any substantive action was taken (in the case of Uganda negotiations were proceeding about the despatch of a fact-finding commission, and in that of Cambodia a report was being made on the situation by the chairman of the Sub-Commission when the government was overthrown). Thus the procedure is still inadequate. But it is a beginning and represents a significant advance on the situation ten years ago when UN bodies discussed human rights only in abstract terms and never concerned themselves with the situations that actually existed in particular countries. At that time communications and petitions were all pigeonholed and never discussed: now the many communications received are examined to see if they give evidence of a "systematic pattern of gross violations of human rights". The task now is to build on what has been developed. It is necessary, for example, to try to speed up the whole procedure so that it can reach final conclusions much earlier: otherwise, as in the case of Uganda, Equatorial Guinea and others, discussion will proceed interminably while thousands of lives are being lost, so that nothing is actually done until the regime has finally fallen. There is also a case for allowing public *reports* to be made by the Sub-Commission, and perhaps by its Working Group, even if the debates remain confidential. It would be valuable to call more senior representatives of governments to appear at the Commission more often. Above all it is necessary to establish better fact-finding machinery so that reports concerning the position on the spot may be made by impartial observers (like the studies made by the Inter-American Commission on Human Rights). Sub-Commissions could perhaps be appointed to look at individual situations; and there could be a role for regional field officers.

There should also be more frequent meetings of the Commission (at least twice a year) so that urgent questions could more easily be raised; or at least the establishment of a small Sub-Commission that could meet at more frequent intervals and in emergencies. Above all there should be much more publicity for the Commission's activities so that the healthy fear that governments are already beginning to have of its reports, manifested in the intensive lobbying they undertake to prevent adverse reports (as by the Argentine Government in recent years), is intensified. This is a matter primarily for the media, but the UN itself can do something through its Office of Public Information; and non-governmental organisations such as UNA can also play a vitally important part in focusing more attention on the Commission's work.

There is another development of the existing machinery which could be of value. There is no doubt that governments are sometimes more influenced by the judgements of bodies which represent governments in their own immediate neighbourhood, of similar political and cultural background, whose opinion counts more for them than that of wider bodies. Already in Latin America the Inter-American Commission of Human Rights probably plays a more effective part in judging and deterring human-rights violations than any UN body. Similarly, the European Commission and Court have been entrusted with much greater power by its member governments than has the UN Commission because they trust its judgement. The steps that would perhaps do more than anything else to improve the protection of human rights in the world today would thus be the creation of regional bodies to perform the same role in Africa and Asia. It would be something if existing organisations such as the OAU and ASEAN were to take more interest in human-rights questions. While this is not a matter on which outside governments can do very much, it could be encouraged by UN bodies (as it was in a recent General Assembly resolution); and again unofficial organisations such as UNA, the ICJ and other such groups have a role to play, through their contacts with sister bodies in those continents, in promoting this development. It is encouraging that there is now active discussion among African states about the establishment of an African Commission.

There has been a great deal of discussion in the UN over many years about the establishment of a High Commissioner for Human Rights. The establishment of an authoritative figure, who could, whenever he received strong prima facie evidence of violations of human rights, ask to examine the situation on the spot and subsequently report, would clearly be a valuable innovation. The difficulty is that, in this form at least, the proposal has become something of a political foot-ball. It has been supported mainly by Western countries and is seen by some developing countries, and even more by the communist states, as evidence of a desire by the West to interfere in their internal affairs. Many countries do not welcome the prospect of a close examination of their arrangements by such a figure. Any proposal that is to have a chance of success must take account of these apprehensions. Though it would be possible for those governments willing to accept the proposal to go ahead by themselves, and hope to draw in others as the system developed, this could probably not be done under the auspices of the UN and there is some danger in creating a divided system. For the moment it might be better to settle for a figure with more modest powers, such as the "Co-ordinator of Human Rights Affairs" that has been suggested by Nigeria. Even an up-grading of the post of head of the Human Rights Division in Geneva (at present Mr. van Boven) to enable him to use his authority more assertively from time to time would do something. But it would help even more if the Secretary-General would lend his own considerable authority to seeking solutions of particularly glaring human-rights violations on occasions. Kurt Waldheim did this usefully in negotiating with Amin for the despatch of a mission to examine the human-rights situation in Uganda. Such initiatives could with advantage be repeated.

We come now to the final objective which we defined: action by individual governments to bring about improvements in the human-rights situation elsewhere.

What are the means available to an individual government in pursuing this aim? What steps can it take to influence a situation that exists in other countries and to persuade another government to mend its ways?

The following are the main types of action which a government can take to influence other states on such matters, in ascending order of urgency:

(a) confidential representations to the government concerned;
(b) joint representations made with other governments;
(c) public statements of concern in parliament or elsewhere;
(d) support for calls in such bodies as the UN Commission on Human Rights for investigation of the situation;
(e) direct initiation of such action in international bodies;
(f) cancellation or postponement of ministerial visits;
(g) restraints on cultural and sporting contacts;
(h) embargoes on arms sales;
(i) reduction in aid programmes;

  (j) withdrawal of an Ambassador;
  (k) a cessation of all aid;
  (l) the breaking of diplomatic relations;
(m) trading sanctions.

This list is not necessarily exhaustive. There are additional grada-
tions that could be introduced at different levels. But it probably includes the main type of response open to governments in dealing with
such questions.

There are many states which rarely if ever undertake any of these
steps. Even Western governments which claim to be concerned about
human-rights questions do not often proceed beyond the first two or
three steps (though the previous Labour government in Britain pro-
ceeded to the last but one in relation to Uganda and the last but three
in relation to Chile).

If action on these lines by outside states is to be effective, there are a
number of conditions that need to be fulfilled. First, the policy must
be pursued consistently, regardless of political prejudice or diplomatic
convenience. This will sometimes involve difficult and unwelcome
choices, both for governments and even more for diplomats. At present our diplomats abroad, perhaps because they are dealing on a day-
to-day basis with a particular set of rulers, tend to become gradually
committed to the existing regime and acquire a marked reluctance to
take any steps which may be unwelcome to them. Equally, they are
most unwilling to have contacts with groups or organisations that are
regarded by those authorities as "subversive" (a former Ambassador
in Iran informed me personally that he regarded it as totally impossible for him to be known to have been frequenting with any forces in
Iran known to be hostile to the Shah during the Shah's day). But the
effect of this policy is questionable even so far as British material interests are concerned; for it means that when a government is overthrown—a not uncommon occurrence in recent times—we are known
as the friend of the displaced and discredited regime and are distrusted
by the incoming government with which we will in addition have had
no previous contacts. But such a policy is even more damaging to our
aims in the field of human rights, because it prevents our diplomats
from having any contacts with those forces that may be doing most to

promote respect for human rights, contacts which may be of great importance to their morale. Britain becomes closely identified with a government that is engaged in seriously oppressing its own people.

So an important condition of an effective human-rights policy (and also perhaps a condition of effective diplomacy) is the establishment of contacts with as broad a section of the population as possible, including political opponents of the government. But there is a corollary for this need for contacts (and one that may be more welcome to foreign office establishments). This is that, even where the human-rights record of a government is appalling, there is every disadvantage in a total severing of relations. This in practice provides the worst of all worlds. Not only is all hope of influencing the regime in question lost, but an isolated regime often becomes still more brutal than before. Equally serious, all opportunity for showing moral support for opposition groups, or influencing the situation in any other way, is also abandoned. By washing our hands of the situation we may feel we are keeping our souls pure. But in practice we condemn the population under pressure to isolation, and ourselves to impotence. We salve our own consciences but abdicate responsibility.

This is illustrated by a number of cases of recent years. Perhaps the most disturbing is the case of Cambodia, where between 1975 and 1978 the most bestial violations of human rights of any in recent years took place, including, it is now believed, two or three million deaths, largely by deliberate killing. Because no Western country had any links with that country during that time, there was not even the smallest possibility of influencing the situation, nor any reason for the Cambodian government to heed the occasional condemnation of its policies that were made in the West from time to time, of which it may well have remained totally ignorant. Indeed the boycotting of the country led to widespread ignorance in the West of what was happening there; so that there was, for example, no upsurge of world indignation until after the regime had already been overthrown and more knowledge of its misdeeds became available. Human-rights violations almost as abominable took place over a number of years in Equatorial Guinea under the Nguema regime, which was equally isolated and equally ignored by Western governments. There is a double disadvantage in such situations. On the one hand, there is little external influence on the government concerned. On the other hand, the oppressed population feels deserted and without recourse. Potential centres of resistance lose hope. Churches and religious groups, without support from elsewhere, lose influence. A policy of isolating a country where such events are taking place is thus the opposite of what in fact is required.

The case for maintaining contacts, however oppressive the government, and however alienated its population, has always been accepted in relation to such countries as South Africa and the Soviet Union, both serious human-rights offenders. It has been generally agreed in those cases that the promotion of contacts provides at least a chance to influence the climate of opinion within those countries, and give support to those forces that are working for change. The same considerations apply equally elsewhere. There is a strong case for deliberately fostering contacts with countries where human rights are being seriously violated. Certain kinds of contact are of particular value in this type of situation. It is, for example, especially important to maintain links with professional, academic and religious groups which are often doing something to keep the spirit of freedom alive. These should be deliberately fostered. It would thus be of great value if the British government were to promote contact between, say, British lawyers and Chilean lawyers; between British scientists and Soviet scientists; between British writers and South African writers; between British trade unionists and Vietnamese or Cuban trade unionists; between church groups in Britain and church groups in Latin America (where the church has often been the main focus for resistance to oppressive regimes). If the existing extensive sponsored-visits programme were deliberately used in appropriate cases to foster contact of this kind, inviting key figures such as politicians, bishops, journalists and others who are fighting a lonely battle of resistance to an oppressive regime, we would perhaps do more of practical value to influence the situation in those countries than by any other possible means. Our information effort may also have a role to play in disseminating the ideas concerning civil and political freedoms which are cherished in our society but knowledge of which is often suppressed in such countries. Non-governmental organisations also have a part to play here; groups such as UNA can play an important part in maintaining links with such groups in other lands. The United Nations Association in Spain was a principal focus of resistance to fascist ideas when Franco was still in power: there is no reason why similar groups should not perform a similar role elsewhere and UNAs in other countries may help them in this task.

Our aid programme too can sometimes be used far more constructively than by simply cutting it off in mid-stream when human-rights violations occur. In general aid should not be provided to governments, in the form of large prestige products which may redound to their glory, but direct to the people. Small-scale assistance can be given, independently of the regime in power, to church groups and others running projects in the field to help those most in need (as the Labour government did to church groups in Chile). It should go primarily to educational and agricultural projects, or small-scale co-operatives, that will make the biggest contribution in creating employment and meeting basic needs, rather than in large-scale dams, roads, steel mills, which bring little direct benefit to most of the population. Where aid is given in this way, and is providing direct benefit to the people, it should not be cut off because of human-rights violations, except possibly in the most exceptional circumstances. It is wrong and illogical that the people of a country, already suffering under an oppressive regime, should be penalised further to punish the sins of their rulers. Moreover, aid programmes may provide a means, however marginal, of influencing the situation through the many direct contacts which result: once it is cut off all chance of influence is lost and the direct contacts with the population are destroyed.

On the other hand, the halting of arms supplies and other kinds of military assistance should be one of the first steps taken once it is established that serious human-rights violations are occurring. On the one hand, such assistance is directly used, or may be so used, by the government in its oppression of its population. On the other hand, it can reasonably be claimed by the recipient government as a mark of friendship and approval. There is thus a need for regular reappraisal of all such programmes to ensure that the human-rights policy of recipient states is satisfactory. Such a policy needs, moreover, to be fully co-ordinated among different organs of the government so that the defence sales section of the Ministry of Defence is not busily peddling arms to a government that may be regarded with disapproval by political departments (this may perhaps avoid the situation reached in 1977 when a proposed arms sale to El Salvador had been almost completed before it was cut off).

The breaking off of trade relations is the most serious step of all that can be taken (it has virtually never been done by a British government for such reasons). It will therefore only be considered in the most extreme cases (it is arguable that Uganda should have been such a case). On the other hand, investment in a country with a bad record could be prevented or at least discouraged at a much earlier stage. Many believe that this should already have occurred in the case of British investment in South Africa. The breaking off of diplomatic relations should be at least equally rare. If, as has been argued, there is always some value in maintaining contacts, it is nearly always best to retain diplomatic representation in some form (especially since once broken diplomatic relations cannot be restored without appearing to grant a mark of approval). If a gesture is required, the withdrawal of an Ambassador, while retaining the rest of the staff, has the necessary symbolic effect without destroying communications altogether.

It is in any case wrong to believe that the most drastic step is always the most influential. Sometimes the most effective weapon is direct representations to the government concerned. Visiting ministers, even if they have arrived for some other purpose—to negotiate a trade agreement or discuss civil aviation affairs—can take the opportunity to make clear the concern caused in their own country by reports of serious human-rights violations, and the obstacle these place in the way of continued co-operation: the minister approached may then use his own influence within the government machine to bring about changes in policies. Visiting foreign ministers should be particularly ready to take up such questions; and even when at home they can express their concern, either about a particular incident or a general situation, to the Ambassador of the state in question. At present, because the basic philosophy of foreign offices is always business as usual, such representations are relatively rare. This allows the erring government to feel that there are few serious political costs to their misdemeanours. But direct representations of this sort can be of special influence. Many governments may be prepared to ride out a critical report or two by Amnesty International. But if made to feel that the whole texture of their international relationships are being affected, they may be more willing to consider seriously radical changes in policy.

Representations on such matters (which will normally be unpublicised, though the wisdom of letting it be known that such a question has been breached can be considered in particular cases) of course carry far greater weight if they come from several governments together rather than from one. This also reduces the political costs of taking action and lessens the problem of *locus standi,* that is, the right of governments to intervene in matters in which their own nationals are not directly concerned (though since Britain and France already in 1863 had no hesitation in sending notes protesting against Russia's treatment of its Polish subjects, there is perhaps no good reason for states to be overconcerned about this question today). In serious cases, therefore, there are good grounds for joining with other like-minded governments in voicing concern and expressing the hope that the situation will shortly be improved. There is certainly a case for far more frequent joint initiatives of this sort than has occurred in the past (they are at present very rare indeed), for they are perhaps more likely to give a government serious reason to re-think its policies than any representations made on a unilateral basis. The EEC has at least once taken such a step (in relation to a Latin American country) but could with advantage do so more often.

A final way in which governments can influence such questions, at least indirectly, is by giving assistance to the many unofficial organisations that are active in this field. These non-governmental organisations are indeed in some ways more effective on this subject than governments. They are able to speak, and certainly to publish, their concern more freely than governments usually do. They are less likely to be accused of political bias, or a desire to score points off a political opponent. And they are more likely to be accepted as reflecting and representing the opinions of ordinary people everywhere. For this reason one of the most useful things that governments can do is to provide assistance for such groups. Financial assistance would not usually be welcomed by them, since they would feel that their independence could be prejudiced, or at least that this might be believed.

But there can be regular exchanges of information and ideas, a pooling of knowledge about the situation in particular states; joint seminars or other activities to educate the public; and co-operation in international human-rights bodies (the last Labour government deliberately cultivated close contacts of this sort with the human-rights "network" of organisations active in this field while, equally important, good contacts existed between Amnesty and similar groups and FCO officials at desk level). It is very much to be hoped that close liaison on these lines will continue. Human-rights organisations will also no doubt wish to maintain regular contact with the new parliamentary Committee on Foreign Affairs to ensure that its members, in considering policy towards particular countries and areas, are at all times very conscious of the human-rights consideration involved. Parliamentarians, and indeed governments, are usually concerned to reflect the views of influential and active groups within the nation; and the more frequent and regular their contacts with human-rights bodies, the more such concerns are likely to be reflected in policy.

The year 1979 should have been seen by human-rights campaigners as a red-letter one. For it has seen the fall of eight governments that were among the worst of all violators of human rights in recent years; these were (in approximate order of brutality) those of Cambodia, Equatorial Guinea, Uganda, Central African Republic, Nicaragua, El Salvador, Iran and South Korea. There were temporary improvements in one or two others (Paraguay, Cuba and perhaps in Argentina). And there was a splendid but unhappily brief example in Bolivia of how the combined action of many brave people, including president, parliamentarians, unions, students and the general public, could, without arms, defeat an apparently successful military coup. But these welcome improvements must also give pause to all those who are concerned about human-rights matters. For it has brought home that in many of these places brutal violations of human rights, including the indiscriminate slaughter of innocent people, could occur over years without any effective action by the international community, indeed to some extent almost unregarded by the outside world. After the defeat of Nazi Germany and the revelation of the unspeakable crimes committed there, many people said that never again would the world sit idly by while millions of innocent people were brutally slaughtered by an insane government. Yet in Cambodia this is precisely what occurred again between 1975 and the end of 1978, while the rest of the world did precisely nothing and few governments uttered a single word of protest. If equally monstrous happenings were to begin elsewhere next year, would the world again stand by, equally dumb and equally helplessly?

One thing that is certainly necessary if outside governments and human-rights organisations are to be more successful in the future is that a greater degree of information should be made available to the public about the situation that exists in different countries all over the world. At present, though most educated people have a vague idea of what is happening in individual countries, impressions are generally very unclear, based on stray newspaper reports rather than reliable and systematically compiled evidence. In practice the degree of concern that is felt about each situation depends almost entirely on how far it happens to have been high-lighted by the press and television. Because there was widespread reporting in Britain about the situation in Uganda between 1975 and 1979, there was general concern in Britain about that country; because there was none about Equatorial Guinea, there was little concern, and almost no knowledge, about the situation in that country though the situation measured in the number of totally innocent people slaughtered was probably even worse. Similarly, because there were only a few and scattered reports about the situation in Cambodia, there was only a slight and sporadic public concern about it at the time when large-scale killings were taking place; and opinion became generally aroused only when the government responsible had already fallen and TV programmes began showing the starvation of the population left behind. Even the best known human-rights organisations in this country during that time devoted far more of their resources (at least so it seems in retrospect) to publicising the situation in Chile and Argentina and the Soviet Union: situations which, bad though they were, cannot be compared with the situation of prolonged and systematic slaughter that was occurring in Cambodia and Equatorial Guinea.

If outside opinions, including outside governments, are to be able to play a more effective role in preventing such outrages occurring again, it is essential that they should be equipped with more objective information about the situation that exists all over the world, and the relative scale of the violations that are occurring. As we have seen, governments usually only take action when their own public opinion is aroused; and a better informed public opinion would do much to stimulate more effective action by governments. The most useful action that could be taken by human-rights organisations—perhaps Amnesty or the so-called human-rights network working together—would be the publication of an annual survey of the human-rights situation in every country in the world (or at the very least all those where human rights are being seriously violated), with some indication of the gravity of the situation in each place. This would not necessarily involve a system of marking (as did the system undertaken for internal purposes by the Labour government until 1979), though it would require fairly bold judgements about the scale of the threats to human life and liberty that were occurring in each state. The task would involve a systematic collation of press reports, and of first-hand accounts from those on the spot in each country. It would need to be done on a systematic and highly objective basis. But it should not be beyond the capability or resources of the organisations working in this field. It would magnify many times the value of the periodic reports at present issued about individual countries, because it would present a comprehensive picture of the world situation so far as human-rights violations are concerned: it would give people an idea of the *relative* seriousness of the problems in different countries of the world; and it would serve to remind people of the *continuing* problems existing in countries that had not perhaps been reported on individually for some years. It would not only be of assistance to all unofficial organisations and individual workers in this field. It would assist governments—and not only in this country—in showing them where they should best direct their own efforts without being accused of political partiality.

Conclusions

We have now examined the problems that occur for governments in seeking to express in their policies the concern that is felt among their populations about human-rights violations elsewhere. When all that is involved is the passing of resolutions and the drafting of conventions, these problems are not great. There may be differences of view between governments about the type of machinery to be established, and the standards to be laid down; but these are not acute political issues and receive little publicity. The difficult problems occur when it is necessary to move on from that process to seeking to influence the conduct of governments in relation to their own populations in their own territories. It is at this stage that many governments feel constrained to pull their punches: because of the danger, in their own eyes, of prejudicing their relations with the governments in question or damaging particular national interests. The natural instinct of nearly all governments, and even more of diplomats, is to maintain smooth working relations with whatever authorities they have to deal, and to avoid injecting into these delicate political issues such as human-rights problems. These attitudes derive partly from the narrow way in which national interests are conceived by many. The wider and more long-term national interests—in bringing about a world in which fewer people are killed, tortured or imprisoned without reason and more enjoy basic freedoms, including the freedom to have a say in the way they are governed; even the less noble one of securing the gratitude of future governments once the oppressive regime has been overthrown, while at the same time winning some respect for demonstrating concern on these questions—these count for little against the immediate aim of not offending existing governments (perhaps a little human-rights training for diplomats, or at least intensive briefing on the question before each foreign posting, would be a help; there is little in the current training of diplomats to lead them to take much interest in this subject). Only if these wider aims come to play a much larger role than they have in the past would governments begin to become more active in the protection of human rights elsewhere.

One of the major tasks for non-governmental organisations such as UNA and others is to ensure that these wider considerations play the role that they should in government thinking. It is important that such organisations should maintain and deepen their links with governments, so that the latter can be made fully aware of the importance that the public, outside official circles, attach to these wider issues. They should seek to foster contacts with officials as well as with ministers (since the former are at least as important in formulating policy), and should insist that they see sometimes the most senior officials (such as the Permanent Under-Secretary and Deputy Under-Secretaries in the Foreign Office), rather than the comparatively junior bureaucrats with whom they often have to be content to deal at present. They should continue to maintain close links with MPs and seek to mobilise these as an effective pressure on governments (parliamentary opinion in this country has so far been a much more muted force in such matters than the human-rights lobby in the U.S. Congress).

Finally, NGOs have a vital role to play in educating opinion at large, including opinion in other countries, and especially in the Third World where there is a less strong tradition of interest in such matters. The organisation of conferences, seminars and other activities, the publication of suitable literature and the maintenance of links with corresponding organisations in other countries all have a role to play here. In the final resort better respect for human rights everywhere can only be brought about through changing the attitudes of world public opinion, and so changing the climate of expectations which ultimately influence governments.

The willingness of Western governments to play an active role in influencing the human-rights situation in other countries too will ultimately depend on their beliefs about the demands placed upon them by their own public opinion. The extent to which, therefore, human-rights considerations play a significant part in the foreign policy of our own government will depend crucially on the success of UNA and other NGOs in building up a constituency within public opinion, at home and abroad, that recognises and insists on the importance of these issues; which accepts that, in today's narrow world, the right of all peoples to live free of oppression, of arbitrary arrest and of torture and sudden death in whatever territory of the world they may happen to dwell is the concern of all of us.